Cooking for Health

ANNE SHEASBY

First published in 1998 for
Tesco Stores Limited
by Brilliant Books Ltd
84-86 Regent Street
London W1R 6DD

Text and photographs © 1998 Brilliant Books Ltd

Origination by Graphic Ideas Ltd, London
Printed and bound by New Interlitho SPA, Italy

About the author

Anne Sheasby has written ten other cookbooks and regularly contributes to several national magazines. She has a particular interest in nutrition and loves to demonstrate that healthy food is often the most delicious.

Photographer	Christine Hanscomb
Home economist	Louise Pickford
Stylist	Antonia Gaunt
Nutritional consultant	Moya de Wet BSc SRD
Recipes tested by	Emma Patmore
	Geri Richards

INTRODUCTION

The recipes in this book have been created and photographed specially for Tesco. They show just how delicious healthy food can be. However, they can only help you enjoy good health as part of a well balanced and varied diet. It's what you eat over the long term that's important! The recipes have been thoroughly tested and all the ingredients are normally available at larger Tesco stores, when in season. There is no need for any special kitchen equipment.

Using the recipes

1 Both metric and imperial weights and measures are given, except for goods sold in standard size packaging, such as cans. As conversions cannot always be exact, you should follow either the metric or the imperial throughout the recipe where possible.

2 British standard level spoon measurements are used. A tablespoon measure is equivalent to 15ml; a teaspoon measure is equivalent to 5ml.

3 Dishes cooked in the oven should be placed in the centre, unless otherwise stated. Tesco advises that all meat, poultry, fish and eggs should be cooked thoroughly. Poultry juices should run clear when the flesh is pierced with a skewer at its thickest point.

4 Some of the recipes include nuts or nut derivatives. These should not be eaten by children, people who have an allergic reaction to nuts, or women who are either pregnant or breastfeeding. It is advisable to check the labelling of any commercially prepared products to ensure that they do not contain nuts or nut derivatives. Recipes that include honey should not be eaten by children under the age of 12 months.

5 Recipes containing sesame seeds or sesame products should not be eaten by children, the elderly or women who are either pregnant or breastfeeding.

6 Vegetables and fruits are medium-sized, unless otherwise stated. If cooking or serving vegetables or fruits with their skins on, make sure that they are thoroughly rinsed.

7 The fat and calorie content of each recipe is given. These figures are for one serving only.

8 Each recipe has a simplicity rating of 1, 2 or 3 chef hats. Recipes with 1 hat are easy; those with 2 or 3 will require a little more effort.

CONTENTS

FOOD AND HEALTH

Our health is affected by what we eat in all sorts of ways and there are some ailments that may require a special diet. This section only gives a general overview of healthy eating and if you have any specific concerns about your health, then you should talk to your G.P.

WHAT'S IN FOOD

Carbohydrates

We need carbohydrate for energy – it really is our daily fuel. Carbohydrates should make up a little more than half our daily calorie intake. Most of it should come from starchy foods like cereals, breads, pasta and potatoes, which are known as complex carbohydrates. These foods supply a steady stream of energy as well as useful vitamins and minerals.

Sugar is an example of a simple carbohydrate, which provides a quick energy boost but no nutrients. Fruits contain natural sugars, but they also supply important vitamins and minerals.

Proteins

Every cell in the body – from fingernails to bones and muscles – needs protein for growth, maintenance and repair. Proteins are made up of compounds called amino acids and anyone who eats a varied diet will automatically be supplying their body with all the amino acids and protein it needs. But, because meat, fish and dairy products are such rich sources of protein, some vegetarians and vegans need to ensure they eat a good variety of vegetables, grains, nuts and pulses to make up their daily requirement.

Fats

If we didn't have any fat in our diet, our bodies wouldn't be able to function properly. In fact, to be healthy, up to a third of all the calories we eat should come from fats. Unfortunately, most people in Britain still have a higher proportion of fat than this in their diet, and a high-fat diet can lead to obesity and an increased risk of heart disease.

Saturated fats, such as those found in animal fats, are most likely to increase the risk of heart disease by raising blood cholesterol levels. Fatty meats and full-fat dairy products are the main source of saturates in our diets. You don't have to avoid burgers, sausages, cheeses, butter and cream completely, just choose lower fat versions where you can. Buy lean meat and half-fat milk, for example, or just spread butter a bit more thinly and have a smaller dollop of cream!

The other fats in our diet – polyunsaturates and mono-unsaturates – may actually help to lower blood cholesterol. Remember though, it's your whole diet that counts. Liquid vegetable oils such as sunflower, rapeseed and olive oil are all high in unsaturated fats. Oil-rich fish such as mackerel, sardines and salmon contain a particular type of polyunsaturated fat (Omega 3) which is also important for a healthy heart. Try to eat oil-rich fish twice a week.

Apart from those people who have inherited high cholesterol levels, cholesterol can usually be lowered through diet quite effectively – largely by cutting down on saturated fats and boosting the intake of soluble fibre. Because it binds with cholesterol, soluble fibre makes it easier for your body to get rid of it as waste – together with the undigested fibre. Fruit, vegetables, wholemeal bread, oats and pulses are all good sources of soluble fibre.

Salt

People who eat too much salt are more likely to suffer from high blood pressure. In turn, high blood pressure is a risk factor for heart disease and stroke. In Britain, the recommended daily intake of salt is 6g (about 1 teaspoon), however, the typical person has about 9g. Salt is made up of chlorine and sodium. If you are concerned about your sodium intake, check the nutrition information on food labels.

EATING A BALANCED DIET

A balanced diet is one that supplies just the right amount of energy and nutrients for your body's needs. Your body will be able to compensate for times when you eat either more or less than usual, but in the long term your diet will be directly reflected by your health.

Eating a healthy balanced diet not only makes you feel good, but it will also help you maintain the right weight for your height and reduce your risk of heart disease and many other ailments. It is now also thought that diet is linked to a third of all cancers. But it is as well to remember, that however healthy someone's diet may be, there can never be an absolute guarantee that they will not get some form of cancer or heart disease.

The easiest way to ensure you have a healthy diet is to ensure it is varied. It may help to imagine a large plate with all the food you eat in a day arranged on it: about a third should be filled with complex carbohydrates (bread, potatoes, rice and pasta); another third should be filled with a good variety of fruit and vegetables – fresh, frozen or canned – that's at least five servings a day. The rest of the plate is filled with other foods: just under a sixth should be meat, fish, poultry, or nuts and pulses: the same amount should be taken up by dairy foods, such as cheese, milk and yogurt – try to choose lower fat alternatives when you can. This leaves a thin portion for fatty and sugary foods like cakes, crisps, fizzy drinks and oils. Of course you may not have all these foods at one meal, but use the idea when choosing foods during the day.

Some foods are thought to be more protective than others especially for certain cancers. Foods which contain antioxidants are beta carotene (the plant form of vitamin A), vitamin C and vitamin E. (See the vitamins and minerals chart on pages 12-13 for the best sources.) Using the nutrition information on food and drink labels will also help you achieve a healthy diet. Even just adding up the amount of fat you eat each day will help you keep the balance right – but try to keep an eye on the sodium and sugar too. Check your intake against these Guideline Daily Amounts, which are for men and women of average weight and physical activity:

Each day	Men	Women
Fat	95g	70g
Calories	2500	2000
Sugars	70g	50g
Sodium	2.5g	2g

Water, drinks and alcohol

Water is essential for life. Adults need 1.6-2.5 litres (3-4 pints) of water a day. However, some ways of drinking it are healthier than others.

Fizzy drinks and squashes can contain a lot of sugar, and should be drunk sparingly. You shouldn't drink excessive amounts of coffee or tea either; they both contain the stimulant caffeine which can lead to insomnia and headaches.

Like most things, alcohol is fine as long as you don't overdo it. A couple of glasses of wine with a meal may actually help to reduce the risk of heart disease, but much more than three or four glasses will have the reverse effect. A man can have three to four units a day and a woman can have two to three, but not every day and it does depend on your size. A unit is one glass of wine, a half pint of medium strength lager or beer, or one measure of spirits. If you do have too much to drink, try to steer clear of alcohol for the next couple of days to give your body the chance it needs to recover.

FERTILITY AND PREGNANCY

Research now shows that the chances of having a healthy pregnancy are significantly increased by eating healthily for at least three months before the baby is even conceived. Women should also take folic acid supplements until 12 weeks into their pregnancy, which greatly reduces the chances of the baby being born with spina bifida. Both men and women should limit their alcohol consumption – excessive amounts are linked to lower fertility and birth defects.

There is no need to eat much more than normal during pregnancy – an intake of about 2400 calories should be adequate. Some additional nutrients are needed though: zinc for the baby's growth and sexual development, and iron to treat or prevent anaemia. An extra serving of bread, cereal, pasta or some other complex carbohydrate is advised, together with the equivalent of a pint of milk (600ml), to meet extra calcium and protein requirements.

Foods to avoid include liver as it is very high in vitamin A and too much of it can harm the baby. Blue or soft cheeses, such as Camembert and Brie, and other unpasteurised foods such as pâtés should also be avoided, as there is a small risk of them being infected by a bacteria called listeria. Eggs, meat, fish and any ready-prepared meals should all be cooked thoroughly to avoid any chance of other forms of food poisoning. Alcohol should be limited to the occasional glass of wine, but try to avoid it altogether during the first 12 weeks of pregnancy.

CHILDREN

Rapid growth means children need proportionately more nutrients than adults. However, because their stomachs are smaller than adults', they need smaller and more regular meals. Young children should not be given low-fat foods, such as skimmed milk – they need the extra calories of the full fat versions. They can have low-fat foods once they are five years old and eating a good varied diet.

Developing good eating habits in children early on will mean they are more likely to eat healthily as they grow up. Try to get children used to the natural flavours of fresh fruit and vegetables, but don't force them to eat foods they don't like. Teeth are most at risk of decay during childhood, so avoid giving them too many sugary foods and drinks.

BEING THE RIGHT WEIGHT

If you're overweight, then you're certainly not alone – more than a third of British people have the same problem. However, the seriously overweight run a higher risk of having high blood pressure, heart disease and cancer, than people of normal weight.

Following a healthy balanced diet within specific calorie guidelines is the best way to lose weight permanently. Women should aim for between 1900-2500 a day, depending on how active they are, while men need 2500-3000 calories. For a sensible weight loss of around 1kg (2lb) a week, aim for a reduction of 400 calories per day. Eat plenty of fruit, vegetables and complex carbohydrates, and cut down on things which are full of empty calories, like sweets, fizzy drinks and alcohol. Avoid fatty foods and grill rather than fry things whenever you can.

Crash-dieting seldom works and all too often its results are short-lived. And faddy diets are often dangerous as they do not provide your body with the full range of nutrients it needs to function properly.

The best way to reach or maintain a healthy weight is diet combined with exercise. Introduce exercise gradually and take advice from a doctor if you have not exercised for a long time. If you do succumb to the odd treat, don't let it upset your long-term goal.

BEING A HEALTHY VEGETARIAN

If you eat a good variety of dairy products, grains, vegetables, cereals and pulses, your diet will supply all the protein you need and be lower in saturated fat and include more fibre than the typical meat eater's.

However, meat is the richest source of several key nutrients, and vegetarians and vegans should take extra care to ensure that they are getting enough iron, vitamin B_{12}, calcium and folate. Beans, lentils, dark leafy vegetables and wholegrain cereals provide iron; fortified breakfast cereals and dairy products are good sources of vitamin B_{12}; soya products, milk, cheese, yogurt and dark leafy greens supply calcium; and most green leafy vegetables, peanuts, fortified breakfast cereals and yeast extract are rich in folate.

Iron deficiency is quite a common problem among women, especially among vegans and vegetarians, in which case supplements may be necessary.

WHAT MINERALS AND VITAMINS DO

Our bodies can manufacture some vitamins and minerals on their own, but others must be obtained from our diet. We all have individual requirements and these change at different stages of our lives. The chart below outlines some of the best sources of the most important vitamins and minerals and briefly explains why our bodies need them.

Minerals

Some minerals, like calcium, are present in our bodies in quite large quantities, while others, like iron and zinc, are needed only in tiny amounts. Minerals help vitamins do their work, but they also carry out many functions of their own – strengthening bones and teeth and maintaining a healthy immune system.

Vitamins

Every vitamin plays a specific part in helping our bodies function properly. For most of us, a well balanced diet will provide all the vitamins we need, making supplements unnecessary. However, expectant mothers, young children, vegans and some vegetarians, the elderly, and people with certain illnesses may benefit from taking supplements. But it can be dangerous to take large amounts of a supplement randomly. If you are in any doubt, it is best to ask your doctor or pharmacist for advice.

Vitamins are either water soluble or fat soluble. Vitamins B and C are water soluble and the body needs to replace them daily as they cannot be stored. Vitamins A, D, and E are fat soluble and can be stored in the liver for approximately one week.

Minerals	Useful sources	Major roles
Calcium	Milk, cheese, yogurt and other dairy products, canned sardines (eaten with their bones), white bread, green leafy vegetables and sesame seeds.	Needed for building bones and teeth and keeping them strong. It is also vital for muscles and the nervous system as well as for blood clotting.
Iron	Offal (liver should not be eaten during pregnancy), lean meat, eggs, fortified breakfast cereals and bread, pulses, dried fruit and leafy green vegetables.	Essential for the production of red blood cells which help to carry oxygen around the body in the bloodstream.
Potassium	Milk, fruits (especially bananas), vegetables, meat, pulses, nuts, seeds, wholegrain cereals and potatoes.	Needed to maintain the fluid balance in the body and to keep the heart rate and blood pressure normal.
Sodium	Occurs naturally in most foods. High levels in table salt, processed meats and many other processed foods.	Needed to maintain the fluid balance in the body. It is also essential for nerves and muscles to work properly.
Zinc	Meat, oysters, peanuts, milk, cheese, yogurt and wholegrain cereals.	Essential for normal growth, wound healing and reproduction. It is also needed for a healthy immune system.

Vitamins	Useful sources	Major roles
A (retinol in animal foods, or beta carotene in plant foods)	Liver (should not be eaten during pregnancy), oil-rich fish, full-fat milk, butter, cheese, green leafy vegetables and brightly coloured vegetables such as red peppers.	Needed for bone growth, skin repair and good vision. It also acts as an antioxidant and helps the immune system.
B_1 (thiamin)	Meat, wholegrain cereals, fortified white bread, fortified breakfast cereals, nuts, pulses and potatoes.	Needed for energy production.
B_2 (riboflavin)	Milk, cheese, eggs, meat, fish, eggs, fortified breakfast cereals and yeast extract.	Needed to release the energy from food and for vitamin B_6 and niacin to work properly.
Niacin (nicotinic acid)	Lean meat, poultry, potatoes, bread, fortified breakfast cereals, wheatgerm and peanuts.	Helps to maintain healthy skin and an efficient digestive system. It is also needed to release energy.
B_6 (pyridoxine)	Lean meat and poultry, fish, eggs, wholemeal bread, breakfast cereals, bananas and nuts.	Needed to make red blood cells, for a healthy immune system and to release energy from protein.
B_{12} (cyanocobalamin)	Lean meat, fish, shellfish, milk, eggs and some fortified breakfast cereals.	Essential for the growth and division of cells. It also helps prevent some forms of anaemia.
Folate (folic acid)	Bread, lightly cooked green leafy vegetables, nuts, citrus fruit, bananas, potatoes, pulses and fortified breakfast cereals.	Needed for making proteins and for passing on genetic information. It is crucial to have plenty of folate before conception and during the first stages of pregnancy.
C (ascorbic acid)	Blackcurrants, citrus fruit and juice, tomatoes, red, yellow and green peppers, strawberries, potatoes and most green vegetables.	Needed for healthy cartilage, bones, skin, gums and teeth and the healing process. It also helps the body to absorb iron and is an important antioxidant.
D (calciferol)	Mostly comes from exposure to the sun. It is also in fortified margarines and cereals, eggs, oil-rich fish such as tuna, salmon and sardines.	It helps the body to absorb the phosphorus and calcium it needs for healthy bones and teeth.
E (tocopherol)	Eggs, nuts, seeds, vegetable oils, sunflower margarines, wholemeal bread and fortified cereal products.	Good for skin and essential for skin repair. It is also an antioxidant.

PLUM TOMATO, LENTIL AND BASIL SOUP

Preparation 30 mins

Cooking 40 mins

Calories 166

Sodium 370mg

Fat 6g

Added sugar 0g

Simplicity

Serves 4

1 Rinse the lentils, drain, then add to a large saucepan of boiling water. Simmer, covered, for 25 minutes or until tender. Drain, rinse and set aside.

2 Meanwhile, place the tomatoes in a bowl, cover with boiling water, leave for 30 seconds, then drain. Remove the skins, deseed and chop. Heat the oil in a large saucepan, add the onions and cook for 10 minutes or until softened, stirring occasionally. Stir in the tomatoes, tomato purée, stock, bay leaf and black pepper. Bring to the boil and simmer, covered, stirring occasionally, for 25 minutes or until all the vegetables are cooked.

3 Remove the pan from the heat and cool for a few minutes. Remove and discard the bay leaf, then purée the soup until smooth in a food processor, liquidiser, or with a hand blender. Return to a clean pan, stir in the lentils and chopped basil, then reheat gently. Serve garnished with fresh basil.

75g (3oz) continental lentils
1kg (2lb 4oz) plum tomatoes
1 tbsp olive oil
2 onions, chopped
2 tbsp sun-dried tomato purée
750ml (1¼ pints) vegetable stock
1 bay leaf
Black pepper
3 tbsp chopped fresh basil, plus extra leaves to garnish

This soup is rich in beta carotene – the plant form of vitamin A – and some of the B vitamins. The lentils are a good source of soluble fibre which, as part of a balanced diet, can help to reduce blood cholesterol levels. They also supply some iron.

It's hard to beat the aromatic combination of basil and fresh ripe tomatoes. Throwing in some nutty lentils makes this soup richer, thicker and more satisfying.

WATERCRESS SOUP

Simplicity 👨‍🍳
Serves 4

Preparation 15 mins
Cooking 35 mins
Calories 143

Sodium 240mg
Fat 5g
Added sugar 0g

1 tbsp sunflower oil

4 shallots, finely chopped

1 leek, thinly sliced

225g (8oz) potatoes, diced

225g (8oz) watercress, chopped

450ml (¾ pint) vegetable stock

450ml (¾ pint) half-fat milk

Black pepper

1 Heat the oil in a large saucepan, then add the shallots and leek and cook gently for 5 minutes or until softened, stirring occasionally. Add the potatoes and watercress to the shallot mixture and cook for a further 3 minutes or until the watercress wilts, stirring occasionally.

2 Stir in the stock, milk and black pepper. Bring to the boil, then reduce the heat and simmer, covered, for 20 minutes or until the potatoes are cooked and tender, stirring occasionally.

3 Remove the pan from the heat and cool for a few minutes. Purée the soup until smooth in a food processor, liquidiser, or with a hand blender. Return to a clean pan and reheat gently, until piping hot. Serve seasoned with coarsely ground black pepper.

Watercress is an excellent source of vitamin C and beta carotene – the plant form of vitamin A. The milk in the soup provides plenty of calcium for healthy teeth and bones.

This quick soup is full of goodness but it looks and tastes sophisticated enough to serve up at any dinner party. For a change, use chopped spinach instead of watercress.

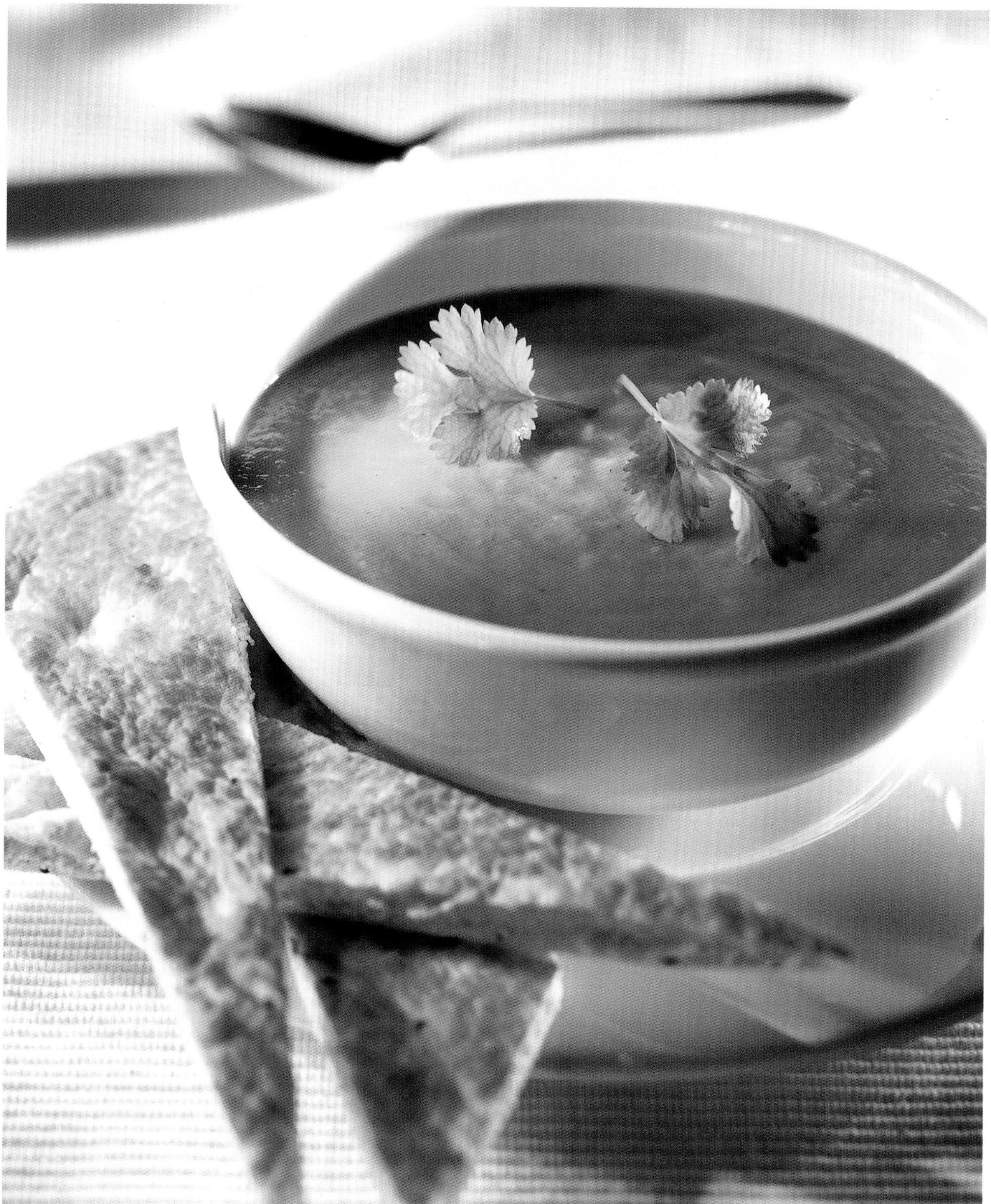

CUMIN-SPICED CARROT SOUP

Preparation 15 mins

Cooking 45 mins

Calories 116

Sodium 360mg

Fat 4g

Added sugar 0g

Simplicity

Serves 4

1 Heat the oil in a large saucepan, add the onion, garlic and celery and fry gently for 5 minutes or until softened, stirring occasionally. Add the cumin and fry, stirring, for 1 minute to release its flavour.

2 Add the carrots, stock and black pepper to the onion mixture and stir to combine. Bring to the boil and simmer, covered, for 30-35 minutes, until the vegetables are tender, stirring occasionally.

3 Remove the pan from the heat and cool for a few minutes. Purée the soup until smooth in a food processor, liquidiser, or with a hand blender. Return to a clean pan and reheat gently. Serve garnished with fresh coriander.

1 tbsp olive oil

1 large onion, chopped

1 clove garlic, crushed

3 sticks celery, chopped

1 tbsp ground cumin

700g (1lb 9oz) carrots, thinly sliced

900ml (1½ pints) vegetable stock

Black pepper

Fresh coriander to garnish

Carrots are a good source of fibre as well as beta carotene – the plant form of vitamin A. The old wives' tale about carrots helping people to see in the dark is partly true; one of the first signs of vitamin A deficiency is night blindness!

This thick carrot soup, spiced with cumin, will really warm you up on a cold winter's night. To get the best flavour, spend a bit extra on fresh stock. Serve with naan bread.

MELON AND GRAPEFRUIT SALAD

Simplicity

Serves 4

Preparation 20 mins
plus 1 hr chilling

Calories 57

Sodium 30mg

Fat trace

Added sugar 0g

1 medium or 2 small melons, such as galia, charentais, honeydew, cantaloupe or ogen

2 pink grapefruit

8 tbsp unsweetened fresh orange juice

1 tbsp orange liqueur, such as Cointreau or medium sherry (optional)

Fresh mint to garnish

1 Cut the melon into segments and remove the seeds. Dice the flesh, or scoop it out using a melon baller. Place in a serving bowl.

2 Slice the top and bottom off each grapefruit and place on a work surface. Using a small serrated knife, cut off the skin and pith, following the curve of the fruit. Holding the grapefruit over a bowl, cut between the membranes to release the segments. Add the segments and juice to the melon.

3 Pour the orange juice and liqueur, if using, over the fruit and stir gently to mix. Cover and refrigerate for at least 1 hour before serving. Garnish with fresh mint.

This salad is rich in vitamin C which plays many different roles in the body – for example, iron cannot be properly absorbed from other foods without it. Orange-fleshed melons, such as charentais or ogen, also supply beta carotene.

If you want a light and refreshing starter, this is it. A dash of liqueur brings out the sweetness of the fruit and if you feel like it, add a few slices of Parma ham.

CHICKEN WALDORF SALAD

Preparation 15 mins
plus 1 hr chilling

Calories 280

Sodium 220mg

Fat 19g

Added sugar 0.8g

Simplicity

Serves 4

1 Place the chicken in a bowl, add the celery and walnuts and stir to mix. Core, then dice the apples and toss in the lemon juice to stop them browning. Add to the chicken and mix well.

2 To make the dressing, mix together the mayonnaise, yogurt, lemon rind and black pepper in a small bowl. Spoon over the chicken mixture and toss lightly to mix. Cover and refrigerate for at least 1 hour before serving.

3 Arrange the salad leaves on serving plates and spoon over the chicken mixture. Garnish with fresh chives.

Chicken and walnuts both supply niacin, which is one of the main B vitamins. Walnuts, like other nuts, are also a useful source of protein and minerals for vegetarians.

175g (6oz) cooked boneless chicken breasts, skinned and diced

4 sticks celery, thinly sliced

75g (3oz) walnuts, roughly chopped

1 red-skinned eating apple

1 green-skinned eating apple

Juice of ½ lemon

200g bag mixed salad leaves

Snipped fresh chives to garnish

For the dressing

4 tbsp reduced calorie mayonnaise

4 tbsp low-fat natural yogurt

¼ tsp finely grated lemon rind

Black pepper

With its fresh lemony dressing, this simple Waldorf salad makes a great starter. To turn it into a deliciously light main course just serve it with some warm crusty bread.

WARM DUCK AND MANGO SALAD

Simplicity
Serves 4

Preparation 15 mins
Cooking 5 mins
Calories 233

Sodium 110mg
Fat 13g
Added sugar 1.5g

1 ripe mango

125g (4oz) mixed dark salad leaves such as baby spinach, lollo rosso and rocket

125g (4oz) sugar snap peas, chopped

4 spring onions, sliced diagonally

2 tsp sesame oil

225g (8oz) boneless duck breast, skinned and cut into strips

Fresh coriander to garnish

For the dressing

3 tbsp extra virgin olive oil

Juice of ½ lime

1 tsp clear honey

2 tbsp chopped fresh coriander

Black pepper

1 Slice off the 2 fat sides of the mango close to the stone. Cut a criss-cross pattern across the flesh (but not the skin) of each side with a sharp knife. Push the skin inside out to expose the flesh and cut the cubes off. Place in a salad bowl with the salad leaves, sugar snap peas and spring onions, then toss together gently to mix.

2 To make the dressing, whisk together the olive oil, lime juice, honey, coriander and black pepper in a small bowl until thoroughly mixed.

3 Heat the sesame oil in a wok or large frying pan, add the duck and stir-fry over a high heat for 4-5 minutes until tender. Add the warm duck to the mango salad, drizzle over the dressing, then toss together to mix. Garnish with fresh coriander.

Mango is a good source of beta carotene – the plant form of vitamin A. It is also rich in vitamin C which helps the body absorb the iron supplied by the spinach.

The rich flavour of duck works particularly well with the sweetness of mango, but you can also use chicken or turkey. Mop up the dressing with some warm pitta bread.

FLAKED TUNA PASTA SALAD IN TOMATO DRESSING

Preparation 15 mins

Cooking 15 mins

Calories 330

Sodium 350mg

Fat 5g

Added sugar 4g

Simplicity

Serves 4

1 Cook the pasta according to the instructions on the packet, until tender but firm to the bite. Drain, rinse under cold running water to cool, then drain thoroughly. Place in a serving bowl.

2 To make the dressing, whisk together the passata, olive oil, vinegar, sugar, basil and black pepper in a bowl until thoroughly mixed. Pour the dressing over the pasta, then toss to mix well.

3 Add the sliced spring onions, yellow pepper, sugar snap peas, sweetcorn and tuna to the pasta and toss lightly. Garnish with the spring onion strips.

> Wholewheat pasta and fresh vegetables are high in soluble fibre. As part of a balanced diet, soluble fibre can help to lower cholesterol levels. It binds with cholesterol and so makes it easier for the body to get rid of it as waste.

225g (8oz) dried wholewheat pasta twists or shapes

4 spring onions, sliced, plus thin strips to garnish

1 yellow pepper, deseeded and diced

125g (4oz) sugar snap peas, chopped

200g can sweetcorn, drained

185g can tuna in water, drained and flaked

For the dressing

5 tbsp passata

1 tbsp extra virgin olive oil

2 tsp balsamic vinegar

Pinch of caster sugar

2 tbsp chopped fresh basil

Black pepper

Pasta, colourful crunchy vegetables and flaked tuna are all bound together in a tangy tomato dressing. Use ridged or twisted pasta shapes as they hold the dressing well.

MARINATED MUSHROOMS ON A BED OF LEAVES

Simplicity 🎩
Serves 4

Preparation 15 mins
plus 2 hrs marinating
Calories 103

Sodium 150mg
Fat 9g
Added sugar 0g

350g (12oz) mixed mushrooms, such as shiitake, large open, button and oyster, thickly sliced

100g (3½oz) baby spinach leaves

25g (1oz) watercress, thick stems discarded

Fresh thyme to garnish

For the dressing

3 tbsp extra virgin olive oil

2 tbsp unsweetened apple juice

2 tsp tarragon white wine vinegar

2 tsp Dijon mustard

1 clove garlic, crushed

1 tbsp mixed chopped fresh herbs; choose from oregano, thyme, chives, basil and parsley

Black pepper

1 To make the dressing, place the oil, apple juice, vinegar, mustard, garlic, herbs and black pepper in a bowl and whisk with a fork to mix thoroughly.

2 Pour the dressing over the mushrooms and stir well. Cover and place in the fridge for 2 hours.

3 Arrange the spinach and watercress on serving plates. Spoon the mushrooms and a little of the dressing over the top and toss lightly to mix. Garnish with fresh thyme.

Mushrooms are rich in potassium, while spinach and watercress are both high in vitamin C. Potassium is needed to maintain normal blood pressure and a regular heartbeat.

Leave the mushrooms to absorb the flavours of the tangy mustard dressing, then pile them onto the spinach and watercress. Warm ciabatta goes well with this salad.

GRILLED VEGETABLE BRUSCHETTA

Preparation 15 mins

Cooking 15 mins

Calories 275

Sodium 670mg

Fat 11g

Added sugar 0g

Simplicity

Serves 4

1 Preheat the grill to high and line the grill rack with foil. Place the pepper, courgette, onion and tomatoes in a bowl. Whisk together 2 tablespoons of oil, the mustard and black pepper, then pour over the vegetables and toss gently to coat.

2 Spread the vegetables in a single layer on the grill rack and grill for 3-4 minutes on each side, until lightly browned. Set aside and keep warm.

3 Toast the bread slices on both sides under the grill and while still hot, rub the garlic halves over one side of each piece of toast. Divide the vegetables between the toast slices, piling them onto the garlicky sides, scatter over the olives and drizzle over the remaining oil. Garnish with fresh basil and serve.

1 red or yellow pepper, deseeded and sliced into strips
1 courgette, halved and thinly sliced lengthways
1 red onion, thinly sliced
2 large plum tomatoes, thickly sliced
3 tbsp extra virgin olive oil
2 tsp wholegrain mustard
Black pepper
1 ciabatta loaf cut into 8 slices, or 8 slices from a baguette
1 clove garlic, halved
8 pitted black olives, thinly sliced
Fresh basil to garnish

> Bread is a great source of starchy carbohydrates and we should be eating the equivalent of at least five slices a day. The vegetables supply vitamin C as well as beta carotene.

This Mediterranean snack is great for drinks parties. Rubbing garlic over the toast gives it a sweet taste that sets off the flavour of the grilled vegetables.

HOUMOUS WITH VEGETABLE CRUDITES

Simplicity 🍳

Serves 4

Preparation 15 mins

Calories 233

Sodium 160mg

Fat 15g

Added-sugar 0g

400g can chickpeas, drained and rinsed

Juice of 1 lemon

3 tbsp extra virgin olive oil

2 tbsp light tahini

1 clove garlic, crushed

½ tsp ground coriander

½ tsp ground cumin

Black pepper

500g (1lb 2oz) mixed vegetables; choose from peppers, carrots, courgettes, cauliflower, broccoli, mushrooms, radishes, baby asparagus and spring onions

1 Blend the chickpeas, lemon juice, olive oil, tahini, garlic, coriander, cumin and black pepper in a food processor, or with a hand blender, until they form a coarse paste.

2 Slice the peppers, carrots and courgettes into sticks, and cut the cauliflower and broccoli into florets. Wipe the mushrooms and trim the radishes, asparagus and spring onions. Arrange the vegetables on a serving plate. Spoon the houmous into a serving bowl and serve with the crudités.

Olive oil is low in saturated fat, but high in mono-unsaturates, which may actually help to lower blood cholesterol levels. Chickpeas contain useful amounts of iron, folate – an important B vitamin – and vitamin E.

Vary the quantities of coriander and cumin to make this Middle Eastern dip as spicy as you like. You can also change the amounts of garlic and lemon to suit your taste.

LAMB AND PEPPER KEBABS WITH CHILLI SAUCE

Preparation 20 mins
plus 2 hrs marinating
Cooking 20 mins

Sodium 160mg
Fat 11g
Added sugar 0g

Simplicity 🎩 🎩
Serves 4
Calories 249

1 In a non-metallic bowl, mix 4 tablespoons of the red wine, the oil, lemon juice, rosemary and black pepper. Add the lamb, turn to coat, then cover and place in the fridge for 2 hours.

2 Preheat the grill to high. Thread the lamb, peppers and mushrooms onto 4 metal skewers, dividing evenly. Reserve the marinade.

3 Place the tomatoes, stock, onion, chilli, tomato purée, garlic, black pepper and the remaining wine in a saucepan and stir. Bring to the boil, then reduce the heat and simmer, uncovered, for 15-20 minutes, until the sauce has thickened, stirring occasionally. Meanwhile, grill the kebabs for 12-18 minutes, until the lamb is tender, turning occasionally and basting with the marinade. Serve with the chilli sauce.

150ml (¼ pint) red wine

1 tbsp olive oil

Juice of ½ lemon

1 tbsp chopped fresh rosemary

Black pepper

350g (12oz) lean boneless leg of lamb, cut into 12 cubes

1 red and 1 yellow pepper, each deseeded and cut into 8 pieces

16 button mushrooms

For the sauce

400g can chopped tomatoes

100ml (4fl oz) vegetable stock

1 small onion, finely chopped

1 green chilli, deseeded and finely chopped

1 tbsp tomato purée

1 clove garlic, crushed

Red and yellow peppers are an excellent source of beta carotene and, weight for weight, they contain nearly three times as much vitamin C as oranges. Lean lamb is a good source of protein, some B vitamins, zinc and iron.

The rosemary in the marinade goes beautifully with large succulent chunks of lamb, while a hot chilli sauce adds some bite. If you prefer, use apple juice instead of wine.

LAMB AND APRICOT CASSEROLE

Simplicity 🎩 🎩

Serves 4

Preparation 15 mins

Cooking 1 hr 45 mins

Calories 374

Sodium 240mg

Fat 14g

Added sugar 0g

1 tbsp sunflower oil

450g (1lb) lean boneless lamb leg or fillet, cut into 2.5cm (1in) cubes

1 large onion, chopped

1 clove garlic, finely chopped

2 tbsp plain flour

1 tsp ground coriander

1 tsp ground cumin

350ml (12fl oz) vegetable stock

150ml (¼ pint) red wine

225g (8oz) baby button mushrooms

1 tbsp tomato purée

1 bouquet garni

Black pepper

175g (6oz) ready-to-eat dried apricots

2 tbsp chopped fresh coriander, plus extra leaves to garnish

1 Preheat the oven to 160°C/325°F/Gas Mark 3. Heat the oil in a flameproof and ovenproof casserole dish on the hob. Add the lamb and cook for about 5 minutes or until browned. Remove and keep warm.

2 Add the onion and garlic to the juices in the dish and cook for 5 minutes or until softened. Return the lamb to the dish with the flour, coriander and cumin and cook for 1 minute, stirring. Slowly add the stock and wine and bring to the boil, stirring. Stir in the mushrooms, tomato purée, bouquet garni and black pepper. Cover and cook in the oven for 1 hour.

3 Stir in the apricots and cook for a further 30 minutes or until the lamb is tender. Remove and discard the bouquet garni, stir in the chopped coriander, then garnish with more fresh coriander.

The leg is the leanest cut of lamb and is also considerably lower in calories than other cuts. Dried apricots are a good source of soluble and insoluble fibre and beta carotene.

Dried apricots give a sweetness to this delicious casserole, but dried pears or peaches also work well. Serve it with some steamed broccoli and bread, rice or jacket potatoes.

BRAISED PORK WITH APPLES

Preparation 15 mins

Cooking 1 hr 30 mins

Calories 242

Sodium 220mg

Fat 11g

Added sugar 0g

Simplicity

Serves 4

1 Preheat the oven to 180°C/350°F/Gas Mark 4. Heat the oil in a non-stick frying pan. Add the pork and cook for 5 minutes or until browned, turning once, then transfer to a casserole dish.

2 Add the shallots and mushrooms to the frying pan and cook gently for 5 minutes or until softened. Add the flour and cook for 1 minute, stirring. Slowly add the stock and cider, stirring until smooth, then add the mustard and black pepper. Bring to the boil and continue stirring for 2-3 minutes, until thickened.

3 Place the apple slices on top of the pork steaks and pour over the sauce. Cover and cook in the oven for 1-1¼ hours, until the pork is tender and cooked through. Garnish with fresh parsley.

1 tbsp sunflower oil

4 boneless lean pork loin steaks or loin medallions, about 100g (3½oz) each

4 shallots, thinly sliced

175g (6oz) mushrooms, sliced

1 tbsp plain flour

200ml (7fl oz) vegetable stock

100ml (4fl oz) dry cider

2 tsp Dijon or wholegrain mustard

Black pepper

2 large eating apples, peeled, cored and sliced

Fresh flat-leaf parsley to garnish

Lean pork generally contains less fat than lamb or beef and is a good source of some B vitamins and zinc. Zinc is essential for the immune system to work effectively.

Pork goes beautifully with the slight tartness of cooked apples. In this succulent slow-cooked casserole the cider brings out the taste of the apples even more.

PEPPERED BEEF STEAKS WITH RED ONION SALSA

Simplicity

Serves 4

Calories 247

Preparation 15 mins

plus 1 hr standing

Cooking 15 mins

Sodium 130mg

Fat 12g

Added sugar 0.1g

2 tbsp mixed peppercorns

4 lean sirloin, rump or fillet steaks, about 125g (4oz) each, trimmed of fat

Fresh parsley to garnish

For the salsa

3 tomatoes

2 tbsp tomato juice

2 tbsp olive oil

1 red onion, finely chopped

2 tsp horseradish sauce

1 tbsp chopped fresh parsley

Black pepper

1 Place the tomatoes in a bowl, cover with boiling water and leave for 30 seconds. Drain, peel off the skins, deseed and finely chop. Put the flesh into a bowl with the tomato juice, 1 tablespoon of the oil, red onion, horseradish, parsley and black pepper and mix together well. Cover and set aside for 1 hour.

2 Preheat the grill to medium. Crush the peppercorns with a pestle and mortar, or rolling pin. Brush the steaks all over with the rest of the oil, then coat with the crushed peppercorns.

3 Place the steaks on the grill rack and grill for 4-5 minutes on each side, until browned and cooked to your liking. Serve with the red onion salsa and garnish with fresh parsley.

Like other red meats, beef is an excellent source of most B vitamins, as well as iron and zinc. Using well-trimmed lean steaks means it can be low in fat too. Tomatoes are a good source of beta carotene – the plant form of vitamin A – and they also supply vitamin C and vitamin E.

The spicy salsa packs quite a punch. It adds a whole new dimension to succulent beef steaks, turning them into a dish that is really modern, colourful and fun.

SPICED BEEF AND CARROT BURGERS

Preparation 15 mins

Cooking 15 mins

Calories 231

Sodium 210mg

Fat 8g

Added sugar 0g

Simplicity

Serves 4

1 Preheat the grill to medium. Place all the ingredients in a large bowl and mix together well.

2 Shape the mixture into 4 round flat burgers, using your hands. Grill for about 10-15 minutes, until the burgers are lightly browned and cooked to your liking, turning once.

Extra lean minced beef has half the fat but just as many B vitamins and minerals as normal mince. The carrots are an excellent source of beta carotene – the plant form of vitamin A – and also provide some fibre.

450g (1lb) extra lean minced beef

2 carrots, coarsely grated

75g (3oz) mushrooms, finely chopped

1 large onion or 3 shallots, finely chopped

50g (2oz) fresh wholemeal breadcrumbs

2 tbsp tomato purée

1 medium egg, lightly beaten

1 clove garlic, crushed

2 tsp ground cumin

2 tsp ground coriander

1 tsp hot chilli powder

Black pepper

These healthy burgers will be popular with all the family. Try serving them in granary baps piled high with crisp salad leaves, slices of tomato and tangy relish.

GINGER AND LEMON CHICKEN STIR FRY

Simplicity ♟ ♟
Serves 4
Calories 225

Preparation 20 mins
plus 1 hr marinating
Cooking 12 mins

Sodium 290mg
Fat 10g
Added sugar 0g

Ingredients
Finely grated rind and juice of 1 lemon
2 cloves garlic, crushed
2 tbsp chopped fresh coriander
Black pepper
350g (12oz) skinless boneless chicken breasts, cut into strips
2 tbsp sesame seeds
1 tbsp sesame oil
2.5cm (1in) piece fresh root ginger, finely chopped
2 carrots, cut into matchsticks
1 leek, thinly sliced
170g pack mangetout
125g (4oz) bean sprouts
1 tbsp dry sherry
1 tbsp light soy sauce

1 In a non-metallic bowl, mix the lemon rind and juice, half of the garlic, and the coriander. Season with black pepper and add the chicken. Turn to coat, then cover and refrigerate for 1 hour.

2 Heat a non-stick wok or large frying pan and dry-fry the sesame seeds for 30 seconds, stirring. Remove and set aside. Add the oil to the wok or pan, heat, then stir-fry the ginger and remaining garlic for 30 seconds. Add the chicken and marinade and stir-fry for 4 minutes.

3 Add the carrots and leek and stir-fry for 1-2 minutes. Add the mangetout and bean sprouts and stir-fry for 2-3 minutes, until everything is tender. Pour in the sherry and soy sauce and sizzle for 1-2 minutes, then sprinkle over the sesame seeds.

> With its skin removed, chicken is a particularly low-fat meat. But it is still a good source of several B vitamins, including B_2 – needed to release energy from food – and niacin, which helps to maintain healthy skin.

The aroma of ginger, coriander and soy sauce will whet the appetites of your family and friends. Make sure you don't overcook the vegetables – they should still be quite crunchy.

THAI-SPICED CHICKEN WITH COURGETTES

Serves 4

Preparation 15 mins

Cooking 10 mins

Sodium 580mg

Fat 6g

Added sugar 0.1g

Simplicity

Calories 172

1 Heat the oil in a non-stick wok or large frying pan. Add the garlic, ginger and chilli and stir-fry for 30 seconds to release the flavours.

2 Add the chicken and Thai seasoning and stir-fry for 4 minutes or until the chicken has coloured. Add the peppers and courgettes and stir-fry for 1-2 minutes, until slightly softened.

3 Stir in the bamboo shoots and stir-fry for another 2-3 minutes, until the chicken is cooked through and tender. Add the sherry or apple juice, soy sauce and black pepper and sizzle for 1-2 minutes. Remove from the heat and stir in the chopped fresh coriander, then garnish with more coriander.

> The skin on chicken contains a surprising amount of fat and calories. By using skinless chicken you can reduce fat by over half and calories by almost a third. The vegetables in this dish supply useful amounts of vitamin C.

Ingredients
1 tbsp olive oil
1 clove garlic, finely chopped
2.5cm (1in) fresh root ginger, finely chopped
1 small fresh red chilli, deseeded and finely chopped
350g (12oz) skinless boneless chicken breasts, cut into strips
1 tbsp Thai 7-spice seasoning
1 red and 1 yellow pepper, deseeded and sliced
2 courgettes, thinly sliced
227g can bamboo shoots, drained
2 tbsp dry sherry or apple juice
1 tbsp light soy sauce
Black pepper
2 tbsp chopped fresh coriander, plus extra to garnish

This stir fry is quick to make and tastes sensational. It helps if you prepare all the vegetables in advance and keep the wok really hot. Serve with rice or noodles.

MUSHROOM AND TARRAGON STUFFED CHICKEN

Simplicity 👨‍🍳 👨‍🍳

Serves 4

Preparation 30 mins

Cooking 40 mins

Calories 207

Sodium 100mg

Fat 10g

Added sugar 0g

2 tbsp olive oil

1 small leek, finely chopped

1 small courgette, finely chopped

1 clove garlic, crushed

50g (2oz) button mushrooms, finely chopped

50g (2oz) oyster or shiitake mushrooms, finely chopped

1 tbsp chopped fresh tarragon, plus extra leaves to garnish

Black pepper

4 skinless boneless chicken breasts, about 125g (4oz) each

1 Preheat the oven to 200°C/400°F/Gas Mark 6. Heat half the oil in a saucepan. Add the leek, courgette, garlic and mushrooms and cook for 5 minutes, stirring, until softened. Remove from the heat and stir in the tarragon and black pepper.

2 Place the chicken breasts between 2 large sheets of baking paper. Beat to an even thickness with a rolling pin. Spread the stuffing evenly over each breast. Roll up, folding in the ends, and secure with wetted cocktail sticks. Brush with the remaining oil and place on a non-stick baking sheet.

3 Cook in the oven for 30-35 minutes, until the juices run clear when pierced with a skewer. Remove the cocktail sticks and cut each roll into 2.5cm (1in) slices, then garnish with fresh tarragon.

> The white meat on a chicken contains more of the minerals phosphorus and potassium than the dark meat, but less iron and zinc. Both types of meat are rich in several B vitamins, including B_6 (or pyridoxine).

The aniseed flavour of fresh tarragon combines beautifully with chicken and mushrooms. Try serving these neat slices with potatoes and some roasted cherry tomatoes.

CHICKEN AND BROCCOLI LASAGNE

Preparation 30 mins	**Sodium** 580mg	**Simplicity** ♟♟
plus 20 mins standing	**Fat** 24g	**Serves** 4
Cooking 55 mins	**Added sugar** 0g	**Calories** 600

1 Put the milk, shallots, celery and bay leaves into a small saucepan and bring to the boil. Set aside to infuse for 20 minutes. Cook the broccoli florets in a saucepan of boiling water for 2 minutes. Drain and set aside. Heat the oil in a frying pan and cook the onion, garlic, mushrooms and courgettes for 5 minutes or until softened.

2 Preheat the oven to 180°C/350°F/Gas Mark 4. Put the sunflower spread and flour in a pan and strain in the milk, then bring to the boil, whisking. Simmer for 3 minutes, stirring. Set aside 300ml (½ pint) of the sauce and stir 100g (3½oz) of the Cheddar, the onion mixture, broccoli, chicken and black pepper into the remaining sauce.

3 Spoon half the chicken mixture into a shallow ovenproof dish. Cover with half the lasagne sheets. Repeat, then pour over the reserved sauce and sprinkle with the rest of the Cheddar. Cook for 45 minutes or until golden.

900ml (1½ pints) half-fat milk

2 shallots, sliced

2 sticks celery, sliced

2 bay leaves

225g (8oz) broccoli, cut into small florets

2 tbsp sunflower oil

1 onion, chopped

1 clove garlic, crushed

225g (8oz) mushrooms, sliced

2 courgettes, sliced

40g (1½oz) sunflower spread

40g (1½oz) plain flour

125g (4oz) half-fat mature Cheddar, finely grated

300g (11oz) cooked boneless chicken breasts, skinned and diced

Black pepper

175g (6oz) egg lasagne verdi sheets

> The milk, cheese, and broccoli in this dish are a good source of calcium. A single portion will also provide a useful amount of vitamin A, together with some of the B vitamins, vitamin C and iron.

This chicken lasagne goes well with a green salad, some warm crusty bread and, if you feel like it, a glass of wine.

TURKEY STEAKS WITH MUSTARD SAUCE

Simplicity

Serves 4

Preparation 10 mins

Cooking 15 mins

Calories 252

Sodium 340mg

Fat 12g

Added sugar 0g

1 tbsp olive oil

4 skinless boneless turkey breast steaks, about 125g (4oz) each

For the sauce

15g (½oz) sunflower spread

15g (½oz) plain flour

300ml (½ pint) half-fat milk

1-2 tbsp wholegrain mustard

Black pepper

Fresh herbs, such as basil, chives or coriander, to garnish

1 Heat the oil in a non-stick frying pan. Add the turkey steaks and cook for 15 minutes or until tender and lightly browned, turning once.

2 Meanwhile, melt the sunflower spread in a saucepan. Add the flour and gently cook for 1 minute, stirring. Remove from the heat and gradually add the milk, stirring until smooth.

3 Return to the heat and slowly bring to the boil, stirring continuously until the sauce thickens. Simmer for 2 minutes, stirring occasionally. Stir in the mustard and black pepper.

4 Spoon the mustard sauce over the turkey steaks and serve garnished with fresh herbs.

Turkey contains less fat and less calories than chicken and is a good source of B vitamins, especially B_{12} (cyanocobalamin) and niacin – one turkey steak provides adults with their entire daily requirement.

Pan-fried turkey steaks served with a simple mustard sauce...what could be easier? New potatoes and lightly steamed leeks go particularly well with this dish.

OVEN-BAKED COD WITH LIME AND FRESH HERBS

Serves 4

Preparation 10 mins

Cooking 20 mins

Sodium 140mg

Fat 4g

Added sugar 2g

Simplicity

Calories 175

1 Preheat the oven to 200°C/400°F/Gas Mark 6. Place the lime rind and juice, lemon juice, olive oil, honey, tarragon, parsley and black pepper in a small bowl and whisk together until thoroughly mixed.

2 Place the cod in an ovenproof dish and pour over the lime mixture. Cover the dish loosely with foil, making sure that it does not touch the food. Cook for 20 minutes or until the fish is tender and starting to flake. Garnish with fresh tarragon and lime slices.

Finely grated rind and juice of 1 lime
Juice of ½ lemon
1 tbsp olive oil
1 tsp clear honey
1 tbsp chopped fresh tarragon
1 tbsp chopped fresh parsley
Black pepper
4 cod steaks, about 175g (6oz) each
Fresh tarragon and lime slices to garnish

Cod is low in fat and calories and an excellent source of protein. But be careful how you cook it – deep-frying a single portion of cod can increase its calories three-fold!

Honey, citrus juice and tarragon turn baked cod into a really special dish, which is incredibly easy to make. Try it with some new potatoes and baby carrots.

CHARGRILLED TUNA WITH PEACH SALSA

Simplicity

Serves 4

Calories 297

Preparation 15 mins
plus 1 hr standing

Cooking 10 mins

Sodium 90mg

Fat 11g

Added sugar 0g

4 tuna steaks, about 175g
(6oz) each

1 tbsp olive oil

Chopped fresh coriander
to garnish

Lime wedges to serve

For the salsa

3 ripe peaches, peeled, stoned
and finely chopped

4 spring onions, finely chopped

50g (2oz) yellow pepper,
deseeded and finely chopped

Juice of ½ lime

1 tbsp chopped fresh coriander

Black pepper

1 First make the salsa. Place the peaches, spring onions, pepper, lime juice, coriander and black pepper in a small bowl and mix well. Cover and set aside for at least 1 hour to let the flavours mingle.

2 Preheat the grill to high. Brush the tuna with the oil and season with pepper. Grill for 3-5 minutes on each side, until the fish is cooked and the flesh is beginning to flake. Garnish with fresh coriander and serve with the lime wedges and peach salsa.

Fresh tuna, like other oil-rich fish, provides Omega 3 fatty acids which are important for a healthy heart. We should try to eat two portions of oil-rich fish a week.

Fresh tuna steaks are a treat on their own, but served with this peach salsa they are absolutely fabulous! The salsa also goes well with ham and pork.

POACHED SALMON WITH ASPARAGUS

Serves 4

Preparation 10 mins

Cooking 10 mins

Sodium 220mg

Fat 25g

Added sugar 0g

Simplicity

Calories 403

1 Place the salmon in a large shallow frying pan and season with black pepper. Mix together the stock and wine and pour over the fish. Add the bay leaves and cover the pan.

2 Bring to the boil, then reduce the heat and simmer very gently for 10 minutes or until the fish is cooked and the flesh is just beginning to flake.

3 Meanwhile, preheat the grill to high. Lightly brush the asparagus with the oil and place on the grill rack. Grill for 5-7 minutes, until the asparagus is tender and lightly browned, turning occasionally.

4 Using a fish slice, remove the fish from the stock and place on serving plates with the asparagus. Garnish with a sprinkling of fresh chives and serve with the lemon wedges.

4 skinless salmon fillets, about 175g (6oz) each
Black pepper
150ml (¼ pint) vegetable stock
150ml (¼ pint) dry white wine
2 bay leaves
20 asparagus spears
1 tbsp olive oil
Snipped fresh chives to garnish
4 lemon wedges to serve

Salmon is an oil-rich fish and contains Omega 3 fatty acids which are important for a healthy heart. Salmon is also rich in vitamins A, B_{12} and D. Asparagus, together with other folate-rich foods, can help to meet the extra need for folic acid during the first three months of pregnancy.

Poaching salmon is really easy and it stops the fish from becoming too dry. You can freeze the leftover stock for up to two months and use it for making soups or sauces.

MARINATED MONKFISH KEBABS

Simplicity 👨‍🍳 👨‍🍳

Serves 4

Calories 118

Preparation 25 mins
plus 2 hrs marinating

Cooking 15 mins

Sodium 20mg

Fat 2g

Added sugar 3g

400g (14oz) skinless boneless monkfish fillet, cut into 2.5cm (1in) cubes

4 button onions or small shallots, halved

1 small red and 1 small yellow pepper, each deseeded and cut into 8 or 12 chunks

1 small courgette, cut into 12 thin slices

Finely grated rind and juice of 1 lemon

2 tbsp freshly squeezed orange juice

1 tbsp dry sherry

2 tsp clear honey

2 cloves garlic, crushed

Black pepper

Fresh herbs, such as rosemary, marjoram and basil, to garnish

1 Soak 4 wooden skewers in water for 10 minutes while preparing the vegetables. Thread equal amounts of the monkfish, onions or shallots, peppers and courgette onto each skewer.

2 Place the kebabs in a shallow non-metallic dish in a single layer. In a small bowl, mix together the lemon rind and juice, the orange juice, sherry, honey, garlic and black pepper and pour over the kebabs. Turn to coat all over, then cover and refrigerate for 2 hours.

3 Preheat the grill to medium. Grill the kebabs for 10-15 minutes, until the fish is tender, turning occasionally. Baste frequently with the marinade to keep the kebabs moist. Garnish with the fresh herbs.

Monkfish is a good source of protein, while being very low in fat and calories. Red and yellow peppers are an excellent source of both vitamin C and beta carotene.

Monkfish is excellent for these kebabs because it has a firm texture and keeps its shape well. The only other thing you need to complete this dish is some steamed rice.

BAKED MACKEREL WITH ORANGE AND ALMONDS

Serves 4

Preparation 15 mins

Cooking 30 mins

Sodium 250mg

Fat 34g

Added sugar 0g

Simplicity

Calories 469

1 Preheat the oven to 180°C/350°F/Gas Mark 4. Make 3 diagonal cuts in the flesh on both sides of each fish, using a sharp knife. Place the fish side by side in an ovenproof dish.

2 Sprinkle the orange rind over the fish and drizzle over the juice. Mix together the parsley and thyme and sprinkle over, then season with black pepper and scatter the almonds on top.

3 Cover the dish loosely with foil so it does not touch the food and bake for 30 minutes or until the fish is cooked and the flesh just starts to flake. Garnish with fresh parsley.

4 whole mackerel, about 275g (10oz) each, gutted and cleaned

Finely grated rind and juice of 1 orange

2 tbsp chopped fresh parsley, plus extra to garnish

1 tbsp chopped fresh thyme

Black pepper

20g (¾oz) flaked almonds

Like other oil-rich fish, mackerel is an excellent source of vitamin D which the body needs to absorb calcium and phosphorus, so it can build strong bones and teeth.

These whole mackerel, baked with fresh orange and almonds, are full of flavour, so serve them with something simple, such as new potatoes and sugar snap peas.

SEAFOOD AND BROCCOLI RISOTTO

Simplicity 👨‍🍳👨‍🍳

Serves 4

Preparation 15 mins

Cooking 45 mins

Calories 371

Sodium 340mg

Fat 6g

Added sugar 0g

Ingredients
1 tbsp sunflower oil
6 shallots, chopped
1 clove garlic, finely chopped
1 red or yellow pepper, deseeded and diced
225g (8oz) long-grain brown rice
500ml (18fl oz) vegetable stock
225g (8oz) chestnut mushrooms, sliced
250ml (9fl oz) dry white wine
400g bag frozen seafood selection, defrosted
225g (8oz) broccoli, cut into small florets
2 tbsp chopped fresh flat-leaf parsley
Black pepper

1 Heat the oil in a large saucepan, add the shallots, garlic and pepper and cook for 5 minutes or until softened, stirring occasionally. Add the rice and cook for 1 minute, stirring, until well coated in the oil.

2 In a separate pan, bring the stock to the boil. Add the mushrooms, wine and 150ml (¼ pint) of the stock to the rice mixture. Bring to the boil, stirring, then simmer, uncovered, for 15 minutes or until most of the liquid is absorbed, stirring often. Add another 200ml (7fl oz) of stock and cook for 15 minutes or until it is absorbed, stirring frequently.

3 Add the seafood and most of the remaining stock and stir frequently for 5 minutes or until the rice is cooked but firm to the bite. Add the rest of the stock, if necessary, and make sure the seafood is cooked through. Meanwhile, cook the broccoli in boiling water for 3 minutes or until tender. Drain well, stir into the risotto with the parsley and season with black pepper.

> Shellfish are generally a good source of low-fat protein, zinc, vitamin B_{12} and niacin. Brown rice contains more minerals, vitamins and fibre than white rice.

The secret to cooking a good risotto is to keep adding just enough liquid and to stir as much as possible. You can use any mixture of seafood – prawns and mussels are good.

TAGLIATELLE WITH TOMATO AND MUSSELS

Serves 4

Preparation 20 mins

Cooking 30 mins

Sodium 300mg

Fat 10g

Added sugar 0g

Simplicity

Calories 488

1 To make the sauce, cover the plum tomatoes with boiling water and leave for 30 seconds. Drain, peel and deseed them and chop the flesh.

2 Heat the oil in a saucepan. Add the onion, garlic, celery, pepper and mushrooms and cook for 5 minutes or until softened, stirring occasionally. Mix in the chopped tomatoes, sun-dried tomatoes, red wine, tomato purée and black pepper. Bring to the boil, cover, then reduce the heat and simmer for 20 minutes or until the vegetables are tender, stirring occasionally.

3 Meanwhile, cook the tagliatelle according to the packet instructions and until just firm to the bite. Stir the mussels into the tomato sauce, increase the heat slightly and cook, uncovered, for 5 minutes or until piping hot, stirring occasionally. Drain the pasta, add to the sauce with the basil and toss well. Garnish with the basil leaves and serve immediately.

> Pasta is low in fat and provides an excellent source of complex carbohydrates for energy. Mussels are rich in vitamin B_{12} which is vital to the health of the nervous system, as well as for the formation of red blood cells.

350g (12oz) dried tagliatelle

225g (8oz) cooked shelled mussels

2 tbsp chopped fresh basil, plus whole leaves to garnish

For the sauce

700g (1lb 9oz) ripe plum tomatoes

1 tbsp olive oil

1 onion, finely chopped

2 cloves garlic, finely chopped

2 sticks celery, finely chopped

1 red pepper, deseeded and finely chopped

125g (4oz) button mushrooms, finely chopped

4 sun-dried tomatoes, soaked, drained and finely chopped

6 tbsp red wine

2 tbsp tomato purée

Black pepper

This homemade mussel and fresh tomato sauce is both quick to make and scrumptious to eat. If you don't want to use any alcohol, you can use apple juice instead of wine.

HARVEST VEGETABLE BAKE

Simplicity 🧑‍🍳

Serves 4

Preparation 10 mins

Cooking 1 hr 15 mins

Calories 154

Sodium 90mg

Fat 2g

Added sugar 0g

1 onion, sliced

2 leeks, sliced

2 sticks celery, chopped

2 carrots, thinly sliced

1 red pepper, deseeded and sliced

500g (1lb 2oz) mixed root vegetables, such as sweet potato, parsnip and turnip, cubed

175g (6oz) mushrooms, sliced

400g can chopped tomatoes

6 tbsp dry cider

1 tsp dried thyme

1 tsp dried oregano

Black pepper

Fresh herbs, such as basil and coriander, to garnish

1 Preheat the oven to 180°C/350°F/Gas Mark 4. Place the onion, leeks, celery, carrots, pepper, cubed root vegetables and mushrooms in a large ovenproof casserole dish and mix well. Stir in the tomatoes, cider, thyme, oregano and black pepper.

2 Cover and bake in the centre of the oven for 1-1¼ hours, until the vegetables are cooked through and tender, stirring once or twice. Garnish with fresh herbs.

People should eat five portions of fruit and vegetables a day and each serving of this dish provides two portions of vegetables. These vegetables are natural sources of the antioxidant vitamins C and E and beta carotene, which may help to reduce the risk of heart disease and cancer.

This satisfying vegetable dish is really cheap, especially if you make it in the autumn when many of the ingredients are in season. Serve it with warm crusty bread.

BEAN, LENTIL AND AUBERGINE MOUSSAKA

Serves 4

Preparation 30 mins

Cooking 1 hr 20 mins

Sodium 320mg

Fat 13g

Added sugar 0g

Simplicity 👨‍🍳👨‍🍳

Calories 370

1 Add the lentils to a saucepan of boiling water, cover and simmer for 30 minutes or until tender. Drain, rinse, then drain again and set aside.

2 Preheat the oven to 180°C/350°F/Gas Mark 4. Meanwhile, cook the aubergine slices in a saucepan of boiling water for 2 minutes. Drain, pat dry with kitchen towels and set aside.

3 Heat the oil in a frying pan, add the leeks, celery, garlic and pepper and cook for 5 minutes or until slightly softened. Add the cooked lentils, tomatoes, wine, tomato purée, beans, mixed herbs and black pepper. Cover and bring to the boil, then simmer for 10 minutes or until the vegetables have softened.

4 Spoon half the bean and lentil mixture into a shallow ovenproof dish and layer over half the aubergine. Repeat. Mix together the yogurt and eggs and pour over the top. Sprinkle over the Parmesan. Cook for 40 minutes or until golden brown and bubbling. Garnish with fresh herbs.

75g (3oz) continental lentils, rinsed and drained
1 aubergine, thinly sliced
2 tbsp olive oil
2 leeks, sliced
2 sticks celery, chopped
2 cloves garlic, crushed
1 yellow pepper, deseeded and diced
400g can chopped tomatoes
5 tbsp dry white wine
2 tbsp tomato purée
400g can black-eye beans, drained and rinsed
2 tsp dried mixed herbs
Black pepper
2 x 150g tubs low-fat natural yogurt
2 medium eggs
25g (1oz) Parmesan, finely grated
Fresh herbs, such as basil, to garnish

Although vegetarians often have a healthier diet than most meat-eaters, they sometimes do not have enough calcium, folate or iron in their diet. This dish provides all three.

Plenty of protein here for vegetarians, and if you're in a hurry to get supper on the table, you can use canned ready-cooked lentils instead. Serve it with a green salad.

ROOT VEGETABLE CURRY

Simplicity 👨‍🍳 👨‍🍳

Serves 4

Preparation 20 mins

Cooking 55 mins

Calories 219

Sodium 290mg

Fat 4g

Added sugar 2g

Ingredients
1 tbsp olive oil
1 onion, chopped
1 green chilli, deseeded and finely chopped
1 clove garlic, finely chopped
2.5cm (1in) piece fresh root ginger, finely chopped
2 tbsp plain flour
2 tsp each ground coriander, ground cumin and turmeric
300ml (½ pint) vegetable stock
200ml (7fl oz) passata
750g (1lb 11oz) mixed root vegetables, such as potato, sweet potato, celeriac and swede, cubed
2 carrots, thinly sliced
Black pepper
Chopped fresh coriander to garnish

1 Heat the oil in a large saucepan. Add the onion, chilli, garlic and ginger and cook for 5 minutes or until softened, stirring occasionally. Stir in the flour, coriander, cumin and turmeric and cook gently, stirring, for 1 minute to release the flavours.

2 Gradually stir in the stock, then add the passata, cubed root vegetables and the carrots, season with black pepper and mix well.

3 Bring to the boil, stirring, then cover, reduce the heat and simmer for 45 minutes or until the vegetables are tender, stirring occasionally. Garnish with fresh coriander.

The vitamin C content of potatoes starts to fall soon after they are harvested and since vitamin C is water-soluble, it is further reduced by boiling. But because the British eat so many potatoes, we get more vitamin C from them than any other food. They also provide fibre and potassium.

This spicy root vegetable curry is based on a traditional Moroccan dish. So, as a change from boiled rice, try serving it with some hot fluffy couscous instead.

SPINACH SOUFFLE

Preparation 30 mins

Cooking 40 mins

Calories 284

Sodium 530mg

Fat 18g

Added sugar 0g

Simplicity 👨‍🍳 👨‍🍳 👨‍🍳

Serves 4

1 Rinse the spinach, remove any coarse stalks or leaves and place in a large saucepan. Cover and cook over a low heat for 4-5 minutes or until it has wilted. Drain and squeeze out any excess water. Chop roughly and set aside.

2 Preheat the oven to 190°C/375°F/Gas Mark 5. Grease a 1.5 litre (2½ pint), 18cm (7in) soufflé dish, sprinkle with Parmesan and set aside. Gently heat the sunflower spread, flour and milk in a pan, whisking continuously, until the sauce boils. Simmer for 3 minutes, stirring. Transfer to a large bowl, add the spinach and mix well. Gradually beat in the egg yolks and 75g (3oz) of the Cheddar, then season with pepper and nutmeg. Whisk the egg whites in a clean dry bowl until stiff (this is easiest with an electric whisk), then fold into the spinach mixture.

3 Spoon the mixture into the prepared dish and sprinkle with the remaining Cheddar. Bake for 30 minutes or until well risen and lightly set.

Ingredients
450g (1lb) fresh spinach
25g (1oz) sunflower spread, plus extra for greasing
1 tbsp finely grated Parmesan
25g (1oz) plain flour
250ml (9fl oz) half-fat milk
4 medium eggs, separated, plus 1 extra egg white
100g (3½oz) half-fat mature Cheddar, finely grated
Black pepper
Large pinch of ground nutmeg

Spinach is a good source of beta carotene, vitamin C and potassium. If you want to help your body absorb the iron in spinach you should include a food that's high in vitamin C, such as fruit or tomatoes, in the rest of your meal.

To give your soufflé an extra lift, place it on a preheated baking sheet just before you put it into the oven.

VEGETABLE CHILLI BAKE

Simplicity 👨‍🍳 👨‍🍳

Serves 4

Preparation 25 mins

Cooking 1 hr 15 mins

Calories 180

Sodium 400mg

Fat 5g

Added sugar 0g

1 tbsp sunflower oil

1 onion, chopped

1 green pepper, deseeded and diced

2 cloves garlic, finely chopped

1 large green chilli, deseeded and finely chopped

2 tsp ground cumin

1 tsp hot chilli powder

400g can chopped tomatoes

1 tbsp tomato purée

3 carrots, cubed

175g (6oz) swede, cubed

175g (6oz) mushrooms, chopped

3 sticks celery, finely chopped

6 tbsp vegetable stock

Black pepper

420g can red kidney beans, drained and rinsed

Fresh coriander to garnish

1 Preheat the oven to 180°C/350°F/Gas Mark 4. Heat the oil in a large flameproof and ovenproof casserole dish. Add the onion, green pepper, garlic and green chilli and cook for 5 minutes or until softened, stirring occasionally.

2 Add the cumin and chilli powder and cook gently for 1 minute to release the flavours, stirring. Mix in the tomatoes, tomato purée, carrots, swede, mushrooms, celery, stock and black pepper.

3 Cover and cook in the oven for 45 minutes, stirring once. Add the kidney beans, cover again and cook for a further 15-20 minutes or until all the vegetables are tender. Garnish with fresh coriander.

The fresh vegetables in this low-fat dish provide a rich source of beta carotene – the plant form of vitamin A, as well as some B vitamins, vitamin C and fibre.

Tempt all the family into trying this tasty vegetarian chilli by piling it into warmed taco shells, or by adding some grated half-fat Cheddar to the finished meat-free feast.

THREE BEAN RICE SALAD

Serves 4

Preparation 15 mins

Cooking 40 mins

Sodium 380mg

Fat 6g

Added sugar 1g

Simplicity

Calories 391

1 Cook the rice according to the packet instructions and until tender. Meanwhile, cook the baby broad beans in a saucepan of boiling water for 4-5 minutes, until tender. Rinse under cold water and drain, then remove the skins if you want. Rinse the rice under cold water, drain and place in a salad bowl.

2 To make the dressing, place the tomato juice, olive oil, vinegar, mustard, garlic, coriander and black pepper in a small bowl and whisk together until thoroughly mixed.

3 Pour the dressing over the rice and stir to mix well. Add the broad beans, black-eye beans, kidney beans, pepper and spring onions and mix well. Cover and refrigerate before serving. Garnish with fresh coriander.

225g (8oz) brown rice
175g (6oz) frozen baby broad beans
400g can black-eye beans, drained and rinsed
220g can red kidney beans, drained and rinsed
1 red pepper, deseeded and cut into pieces
1 bunch spring onions, chopped
Fresh coriander to garnish

For the dressing

150ml (¼ pint) tomato juice
1 tbsp olive oil
1 tbsp white wine vinegar
2 tsp Dijon mustard
1 clove garlic, crushed
2 tbsp chopped fresh coriander
Black pepper

Its combination of rice and beans makes this dish a good source of protein. Beans and other pulses provide several minerals and most B vitamins, and because they contain soluble fibre, they may help to reduce blood cholesterol.

It's the tomato dressing which really makes this brown rice and bean salad taste so good. If you want to serve it warm, rinse the rice in boiling water before dressing it.

LINGUINE WITH LEEKS AND MUSHROOMS

Simplicity ♟♟

Serves 4

Preparation 10 mins

Cooking 15 mins

Calories 484

Sodium 160mg

Fat 14g

Added sugar 0g

500g (1lb 2oz) leeks, sliced

275g (10oz) button mushrooms, sliced

1 bay leaf

40g (1½oz) sunflower spread

40g (1½oz) plain flour

500ml (18fl oz) half-fat milk

2 tbsp snipped fresh chives, plus extra to garnish

Black pepper

500g pack fresh linguine or tagliatelle

1 Steam the leeks and mushrooms with the bay leaf over a saucepan of boiling water for 10-15 minutes, until tender. Discard the bay leaf and keep the vegetables warm.

2 Melt the sunflower spread in a pan, add the flour and cook gently for 1 minute, stirring. Remove from the heat and gradually add the milk. Return to the heat and bring to the boil, stirring, until thickened. Reduce the heat and simmer for 2 minutes, stirring. Add the vegetables, chives and black pepper and heat through.

3 Meanwhile, cook the pasta according to the packet instructions, and until firm to the bite. Drain and return to the pan, then add the leek and mushroom sauce and toss lightly to mix. Garnish with fresh chives.

Leeks provide some folate, but in this dish it is the milk that supplies most of the nutrients. Apart from having less vitamin A, half-fat milk has all the nutrients of full-fat milk.

This creamy leek and mushroom sauce is especially good with linguine or tagliatelle but you could experiment with other fresh pastas. Serve it with ciabatta and a big salad.

RED ONION, COURGETTE AND TOMATO PIZZA

Serves 4

Preparation 25 mins

Cooking 35 mins

Sodium 620mg

Fat 19g

Added sugar 1g

Simplicity

Calories 425

1 Preheat the oven to 220°C/425°F/Gas Mark 7. Heat the oil in a saucepan, then add the onions, pepper, courgettes and garlic and cook for 5 minutes or until softened, stirring occasionally. Set aside.

2 Place the flour and baking powder in a bowl, then rub in the sunflower spread. Stir in the milk to form a smooth dough and knead lightly.

3 Roll out the dough on a lightly floured surface to a circle about 25cm (10in) wide and place on a greased baking sheet. Mix together the passata, tomato purée, mixed herbs and black pepper and spread over the dough. Top with the onion mixture.

4 Arrange the tomato slices on top and sprinkle with Cheddar. Bake for 25-30 minutes, until the cheese is golden brown and bubbling. Garnish with fresh basil if using.

1 tbsp olive oil, plus extra for greasing

2 small red onions, sliced

1 yellow pepper, deseeded and sliced

2 small courgettes, sliced

1 clove garlic, crushed

225g (8oz) plain wholemeal flour

2 tsp baking powder

50g (2oz) sunflower spread

100ml (4fl oz) half-fat milk

4 tbsp passata

1 tbsp tomato purée

2 tsp dried mixed herbs

Black pepper

3 small plum tomatoes, sliced

100g (3½oz) half-fat mature Cheddar, grated

Fresh basil to garnish (optional)

The wholemeal flour in the dough provides complex carbohydrates and with the vegetables and cheese, this pizza makes a nourishing and well-balanced meal.

The red onions start to caramelise and become quite sweet while the pizza is cooking. If you don't have any mixed herbs, use dried oregano or marjoram instead.

GREEN BEANS WITH WALNUT DRESSING

Simplicity

Serves 4-6

Preparation 5 mins

Cooking 6 mins

Calories 104

Sodium 40mg

Fat 9g

Added sugar 0g

450g (1lb) fine green beans
2 tbsp walnut oil
1 tbsp olive oil
1 tbsp white wine vinegar
1 tsp Dijon mustard
Black pepper

1 Cook the beans in a saucepan of boiling water for 5-6 minutes, until tender.

2 Meanwhile, put the walnut oil, olive oil, vinegar, mustard and black pepper in a small bowl and mix together thoroughly. Drain the beans and serve hot or cold with the dressing drizzled over.

> Green beans and green leafy vegetables are good sources of folate (or folic acid), one of the most important vitamins for women to take before conception and during early pregnancy; it greatly reduces the risk of babies being born with spina bifida or other neural tube defects.

This delicious nutty dressing is great with green beans, but it works just as well with a variety of cooked vegetables, including cauliflower, baby courgettes and mushrooms.

SWEET POTATO PUREE

Serves 4

Preparation 10 mins

Cooking 15 mins

Sodium 150mg

Fat 3g

Added sugar 0g

Simplicity

Calories 200

1 Cook the sweet potatoes in a saucepan of boiling water for 10-15 minutes, until tender. Drain thoroughly, then mash until very smooth.

2 Heat the milk in a saucepan, then add to the potato with the garlic, Cheddar, parsley, chives and black pepper. Beat until smooth and well mixed, then serve hot, garnished with fresh chives.

750g (1lb 11oz) sweet potatoes, cut into large chunks

3 tbsp full-fat milk

1 clove garlic, crushed

40g (1½oz) half-fat mature Cheddar, finely grated

1 tbsp chopped fresh parsley

1 tbsp snipped fresh chives, plus extra to garnish

Black pepper

Unlike normal potatoes, the orange-fleshed sweet potato is an excellent source of beta carotene – the plant form of vitamin A. It also provides some potassium and vitamin C.

Strictly speaking, this is a side dish but the cheese and herbs make it so good you may not want to eat anything else other than some warm bread and a salad.

ROASTED SHALLOTS WITH ROSEMARY

Simplicity

Serves 4

Preparation 5 mins

Cooking 40 mins

Calories 88

Sodium 110mg

Fat 6g

Added sugar 0g

600g (1lb 5oz) shallots or pickling onions

2 tbsp olive oil

1-2 tbsp chopped fresh rosemary

Black pepper

1 Preheat the oven to 200°C/400°F/Gas Mark 6. Place the shallots in a roasting tin, drizzle over the oil, sprinkle with the rosemary and black pepper, then toss to mix well.

2 Cook in the oven for 30-40 minutes, until the shallots are tender and golden brown, stirring once or twice. Serve hot.

Shallots, like onions, are very low in calories, so you can afford to add a little oil – especially one that is low in saturates like olive oil.

Something miraculous happens when shallots are roasted; they become much milder and really sweet. Next time you're doing a Sunday roast, give them a go.

MANGETOUT AND CARROTS WITH SESAME SEEDS

Serves 4

Preparation 10 mins

Cooking 5 mins

Sodium 120mg

Fat 8g

Added sugar 0g

Simplicity

Calories 120

1 Peel the cucumber, cut it in half lengthways and scoop out the seeds. Slice into half moons.

2 Heat a non-stick wok or large frying pan. Add the sesame seeds and dry-fry for 1 minute or until toasted, tossing constantly. Remove and set aside. Add the oil, then the cucumber and carrots and stir-fry over a high heat for 2 minutes. Add the mangetout and spring onions and stir-fry for a further 2-3 minutes, until all the vegetables are cooked but still crisp.

3 Sprinkle over the lemon juice and sesame seeds, toss to mix and stir-fry for a few seconds to heat through. Season with pepper and serve.

½ cucumber
2 tbsp sesame seeds
1 tbsp sunflower oil
4 carrots, cut into matchsticks
225g (8oz) mangetout
6 spring onions, chopped
1 tbsp lemon juice
Black pepper

Both carrots and mangetout are a good source of beta carotene – the plant form of vitamin A. Mangetout are also a rich source of vitamin C. Both vegetables supply fibre.

A handful of toasted sesame seeds makes all the difference to this simple stir fry. If you like a more oriental flavour, use lime juice instead of lemon.

RASPBERRY YOGURT ICE

Simplicity 👨‍🍳

Serves 4

Calories 158

Preparation 15 mins
plus 6 hrs freezing and
30 mins chilling

Sodium 70mg

Fat 1g

Added sugar 20g

350g (12oz) raspberries,
defrosted if frozen

50g (2oz) caster sugar

300g (11oz) low-fat
raspberry yogurt

125g (4oz) virtually fat-free
Greek yogurt

Fresh mint and raspberries
to decorate

1 Place the raspberries in a food processor and blend until smooth, or use a hand blender. Press the mixture through a sieve into a bowl, discarding the pips, then add the sugar and mix well.

2 Mix in the raspberry yogurt and Greek yogurt. Pour the mixture into a shallow freezer container, cover, and freeze for 2 hours. Meanwhile, put a large empty bowl into the refrigerator to chill.

3 Spoon the raspberry mixture into the chilled bowl and beat with a fork or whisk until smooth to break down the ice crystals. Return to the container, cover, and freeze for a further 4 hours or until firm.

4 Transfer to the fridge for 30 minutes before serving to soften. Serve in scoops, decorated with fresh mint and raspberries.

Fresh raspberries are rich in vitamin C, while the yogurt provides a good source of calcium. Using virtually fat-free Greek yogurt also helps to keep down the calories.

The unmistakable flavour of raspberries works really well in this tangy ice but there is nothing to stop you using fresh strawberries and strawberry yogurt instead.

GRILLED HONEYED FRUIT WITH VANILLA YOGURT

Serves 4-6

Preparation 15 mins

Cooking 20 mins

Sodium 70mg

Fat 5g

Added sugar 12g

Simplicity

Calories 243

1 Preheat the grill to high. In a bowl, mix together 2 tablespoons of the honey with the apple juice and mixed spice. Peel the mango and slice the flesh off the stone.

2 Cover the grill rack with foil and lay half the mango, pineapple, apple and pear slices on it. Drizzle over half the honeyed spice mixture. Grill for 10 minutes or until slightly softened, turning the fruit once. Keep warm while you repeat with the remaining fruit and honey mixture.

3 Meanwhile, place the Greek yogurt and plain yogurt in a bowl with the vanilla extract or essence and the remaining honey, then mix well. Serve the fruit warm with the vanilla yogurt.

3 tbsp clear honey
2 tbsp unsweetened apple juice
1 tsp ground mixed spice
1 ripe mango
1 small pineapple, peeled, cored and sliced
2 eating apples, peeled, cored and sliced
2 pears, peeled, cored and sliced
175g (6oz) Greek yogurt
150g (5oz) low-fat plain yogurt
Few drops of natural vanilla extract or vanilla essence

Pineapple, mango, apples and pears all supply vitamin C and fibre. Mango is also rich in beta carotene and both types of yogurt are a good source of calcium.

Fruit drizzled with honey and grilled until it just starts to brown is wonderful served warm with ice cream. But it's better still with vanilla yogurt spooned over it.

LEMON AND SULTANA BREAD PUDDING

Simplicity 👨‍🍳

Serves 4-6

Calories 424

Preparation 15 mins
plus 30 mins standing

Cooking 45 mins

Sodium 500mg

Fat 15g

Added sugar 10g

40g (1½oz) sunflower spread, plus extra for greasing

6 medium slices wholemeal bread

125g (4oz) sultanas

Finely grated rind of 1 small lemon

40g (1½oz) soft light brown sugar

2 medium eggs

600ml (1 pint) half-fat milk

---

1 Lightly grease a 23 x 28cm (9 x 11in) ovenproof dish. Spread one side of each bread slice with sunflower spread, then cut each slice into 4 triangles and arrange half of them in the base of the prepared dish, spread-side up.

2 Mix together the sultanas, lemon rind and half the sugar, then sprinkle over the bread. Arrange the remaining bread over the top, spread-side up, and sprinkle with the rest of the sugar.

3 Beat together the eggs and milk and pour over the bread. Set aside for 30 minutes to allow the bread to absorb some of the liquid. Meanwhile, preheat the oven to 180°C/350°F/Gas Mark 4. Bake in the oven for 45 minutes, until lightly set and golden brown.

> Wholemeal bread is a much better source of B vitamins, iron, zinc and fibre than white bread. However, white bread is fortified with calcium by law and contains twice as much of the mineral as wholemeal bread.

The smell of this freshly made lemony bread pudding baking in the oven is quite irresistible. If you serve it with low-fat custard, you can even have guilt-free seconds.

BLUEBERRY AND APPLE OATMEAL CRUMBLE

Serves 4

Preparation 15 mins

Cooking 45 mins

Calories 360

Fat 15g

Added sugar 17g

Simplicity

Sodium 110mg

1 Preheat the oven to 180°C/350°F/Gas Mark 4. Place the flour, oatmeal and almonds in a bowl and stir to mix. Lightly rub in the sunflower spread until the mixture resembles breadcrumbs. Stir in the sugar and cinnamon.

2 Place the apples and blueberries in a 16 x 23cm (6½ x 9in) ovenproof dish. Mix together the apple juice and honey, pour over the apples and blueberries and stir gently to mix.

3 Spoon the crumble mixture evenly over the fruit so that it is completely covered. Bake for 40-45 minutes, until golden brown.

75g (3oz) plain wholemeal flour
50g (2oz) medium oatmeal
25g (1oz) ground almonds
50g (2oz) sunflower spread
50g (2oz) soft light brown sugar
1 tsp ground cinnamon
3 eating apples, peeled, cored and thinly sliced
225g (8oz) fresh blueberries
2 tbsp unsweetened apple juice
1 tbsp clear honey

Blueberries supply some vitamin C, and like cranberries, they contain antibacterial compounds which can help to combat cystitis. And because they are naturally sweet, they do not need to be sweetened with too much sugar.

You can try using raspberries or sliced peaches instead of blueberries in this crunchy, fruit-packed crumble. Serve it with low-fat custard, Greek yogurt or ice cream.

CHOCOLATE AND STRAWBERRY ROULADE

Simplicity 👨‍🍳👨‍🍳👨‍🍳

Serves 6

Calories 346

Preparation 25 mins

Cooking 12 mins

plus 20 mins cooling

Sodium 150mg

Fat 9g

Added sugar 34g

Sunflower spread for greasing

3 medium eggs

125g (4oz) caster sugar

50g (2oz) plain wholemeal flour

50g (2oz) plain white flour, sifted

15g (½oz) cocoa powder, sifted, plus 2 tsp to dust

125g (4oz) Greek yogurt

100g (3½oz) virtually fat-free fromage frais

150g (5oz) strawberries, sliced or chopped

Icing sugar to dust

1 Preheat the oven to 200°C/400°F/Gas Mark 6. Grease a 33 x 23cm (13 x 9in) swiss roll tin and line with non-stick baking paper. Put the eggs and sugar into a heatproof bowl over a saucepan of simmering water and whisk until pale and creamy. Remove from the heat and whisk until cool.

2 Lightly fold the wholemeal flour into the mixture using a metal spoon, then fold in the white flour and cocoa powder with 1 tablespoon of hot water. Pour into the tin and smooth the surface with the back of a spoon.

3 Bake for 10-12 minutes, until risen and firm. Turn out onto a sheet of non-stick baking paper, trim the edges of the sponge with a sharp knife and roll up with the paper inside. Place seam-side down on a wire rack and leave to cool for 30 minutes, then carefully unroll and discard the paper.

4 Mix together the Greek yogurt and fromage frais and spread evenly over the cake. Scatter over the strawberries, then roll up the cake. Dust with cocoa powder and icing sugar.

Strawberries have one of the highest vitamin C contents of any fruit and there are only 30 calories in a typical serving.

Fresh raspberries, sliced peaches, pears or bananas can also be used to fill this irresistibly light chocolate sponge.

DATE AND ORANGE OATMEAL COOKIES

Makes 45 cookies

Preparation 15 mins

Cooking 15 mins

Sodium 30mg each

Fat 3g each

Added sugar 3g each

Simplicity

Calories 64 each

1 Preheat the oven to 180°C/350°F/Gas Mark 4. Line 2 large baking sheets with non-stick baking paper. Place the sugars and sunflower spread in a bowl and beat together until light and fluffy. Add the orange rind, then gradually beat in the egg.

2 Fold in the flour and oatmeal, then fold in the dates and mix until well blended.

3 Place heaped teaspoonfuls of the mixture onto the baking sheets, spacing well apart to allow the cookies to spread during baking. Bake in the oven for 15 minutes or until golden brown.

4 Cool slightly on the baking sheets, then transfer to a wire rack to cool completely.

75g (3oz) light soft brown sugar

75g (3oz) caster sugar

150g (5oz) sunflower spread

Finely grated rind of 1 orange

1 medium egg

150g (5oz) self-raising wholemeal flour

75g (3oz) medium oatmeal

125g (4oz) dried dates, finely chopped

Dried dates are a good source of potassium and contain useful amounts of fibre, making them a gentle but effective laxative. Oatmeal also contains soluble fibre and is therefore thought to be helpful in reducing blood cholesterol.

These crumbly, fruity oatmeal cookies keep well in an airtight container and can be stored in the freezer for up to two months – if you can resist them that long.

FRESH STRAWBERRY SCONES

Simplicity

Makes 12 scones

Preparation 15 mins

Cooking 10 mins

Calories 104 each

Sodium 120mg each

Fat 4g each

Added sugar 2g each

225g (8oz) self-raising wholemeal flour

1 tsp baking powder

Pinch of salt

50g (2oz) sunflower spread

25g (1oz) caster sugar

100g (3½oz) fresh strawberries, chopped

100ml (4fl oz) half-fat milk, plus extra for glazing

1 Preheat the oven to 220°C/425°F/Gas Mark 7. Put the flour, baking powder and salt in a large bowl and stir to mix. Lightly rub in the sunflower spread until the mixture resembles breadcrumbs.

2 Mix in the sugar and strawberries, then add enough milk to form a soft dough. Turn the dough out onto a floured surface, knead lightly, then carefully roll to a thickness of 2cm (¾in).

3 Cut out 12 rounds, using a 5cm (2in) pastry cutter, and place on a baking sheet. Brush with milk to glaze. Bake in the oven for 8-10 minutes, until well risen and golden brown. Transfer to a wire rack to cool.

> Wholemeal flour is a good source of fibre, and supplies some of the B vitamins, iron, zinc and vitamin E, while strawberries are an excellent source of vitamin C.

To give these traditional scones a warm, spicy flavour, add a teaspoon of ground cinnamon to the flour at the start of this recipe. Serve with crème fraîche and strawberries.

SPICED APPLE MUFFINS

Makes 9 muffins

Preparation 20 mins

Cooking 20 mins

Sodium 310mg each

Fat 6g each

Added sugar 6g each

Simplicity 👨‍🍳 👨‍🍳

Calories 161 each

1 Preheat the oven to 200°C/400°F/Gas Mark 6. Line a muffin or deep bun tin with 9 muffin cases and set aside. Place the flour, baking powder, mixed spice and salt in a bowl and mix well.

2 In a separate large bowl, mix together the sugar, egg, milk and the melted sunflower spread, then gently fold in the flour mixture – just enough to combine them. (The mixture should look quite lumpy; it will produce heavy muffins if overmixed.) Gently fold in the apple.

3 Divide the mixture between the muffin cases. Bake in the oven for 20 minutes or until risen and golden brown. Transfer to a wire rack to cool.

200g (7oz) plain wholemeal flour
1 tbsp baking powder
1½ tsp ground mixed spice
Pinch of salt
50g (2oz) light soft brown sugar
1 medium egg, beaten
200ml (7fl oz) half-fat milk
50g (2oz) sunflower spread, melted
1 cooking apple, peeled, cored and chopped

Cooking apples contain useful amounts of vitamin C, while both eating apples and cooking apples are a good source of soluble fibre which can help to reduce cholesterol levels.

The problem with these muffins is that they smell so good when they come out of the oven, they may not last until tea time! Serve them on their own with a cup of tea.

BANANA AND HONEY TEA BREAD

Simplicity 👨‍🍳

Makes 8-10 slices

Preparation 20 mins

Cooking 1 hr 15 mins

Calories 368 each

Sodium 200mg each

Fat 15g each

Added sugar 28g each

125g (4oz) sunflower spread, plus extra for greasing

125g (4oz) light soft brown sugar

125g (4oz) set honey

2 medium eggs, beaten

225g (8oz) self-raising wholemeal flour

1 tsp ground nutmeg

3 bananas

Lemon juice

1 Preheat the oven to 180°C/350°F/Gas Mark 4. Lightly grease and line a 900g (2lb) loaf tin. Beat together the sunflower spread, sugar and honey in a bowl until light and fluffy. Gradually beat in the eggs, then fold in the flour and nutmeg.

2 Mash the bananas with a little lemon juice and fold them into the mixture until thoroughly combined. Spoon the mixture into the prepared tin and level the surface with the back of a spoon.

3 Bake for 1-1¼ hours or until risen, golden and firm to the touch. If necessary, cover lightly with baking paper or foil towards the end of cooking to prevent the top of the bread overbrowning.

4 Cool for a few minutes in the tin, then turn out onto a wire rack and leave to cool completely.

Ripe bananas are easily digested and quickly release their natural sugars into the bloodstream which is why many athletes eat them during competitions. They are also high in potassium which helps to maintain normal blood pressure.

This moist banana loaf can be served warm or cold. But best of all, toast it to make a great pudding or tea time treat. For a lighter loaf, use white self-raising flour.

INDEX

The Tesco Cookery Series

Fast Family Meals • Great Value Meals • Fast Fresh Food • Fun Food for Children
Pasta • Fish and Shellfish • Mainly Vegetables • Meat and Poultry • Puddings
Best of British • Mediterranean Food • Tastes of the Orient

The Lifestyle Collection

Cooking for Health • Entertaining • The Essential Cookbook • Food for Friends